BRIXHAM

Part II

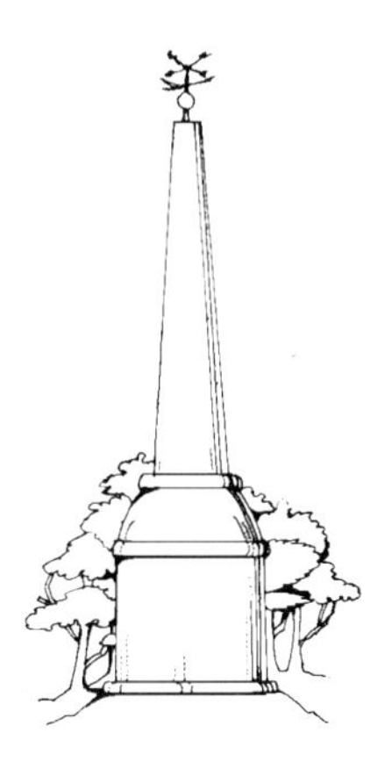

Other Titles in This Series

Brixham of Yesteryear, Parts I and III, *Chips Barber*
Beesands and Hallsands of Yesteryear, *Cyril Courtney*
Ashburton of Yesteryear, *John Germon and Pete Webb*
The Teign Valley of Yesteryear, Parts I and II, *Chips Barber*
Pinhoe of Yesteryear, Parts I and II, *Chips Barber*
Kingsteignton of Yesteryear, *Richard Harris*
Heavitree of Yesteryear, *Chips Barber* • Ide of Yesteryear, *Mavis Piller*
Kenton and Starcross of Yesteryear, *Eric Vaughan*
Princetown of Yesteryear, Parts I and II, *Chips Barber*
Exmouth Century, Parts One and Two, *George Pridmore*
Withycombe Raleigh of Yesteryear, Parts I and II, *Stocker/Gardner/Long/Southwell*
Exmouth of Yesteryear, *Kevin Palmer* • Littleham of Yesteryear, *Kevin Palmer*
Sampford Peverell of Yesteryear, *Bridget Bernhardt and Jenny Holley*
Sidmouth of Yesteryear, *Chips Barber* • Crediton of Yesteryear, *Victoria Labbett*
St Thomas of Yesteryear, Parts I, II and III, *Mavis Piller*
Whipton of Yesteryear, *Chips Barber and Don Lashbrook*
Dawlish of Yesteryear, *Chips Barber* • Torquay of Yesteryear, *Leslie Retallick*
Devon's Railways of Yesteryear, *Chips Barber*
Kingskerswell of Yesteryear, *Chips Barber and John Hand*
Chagford of Yesteryear, *Chips Barber* • Dartmoor of Yesteryear, *Chips Barber*
Okehampton of Yesteryear, *Mike and Hilary Wreford*
Lympstone of Yesteryear, *Anne Scott* • Exminster of Yesteryear, *Chips Barber*
Whitchurch of Yesteryear, *Chips Barber* • Dartmouth of Yesteryear, *Chips Barber*
Burgh Island and Bigbury Bay of Yesteryear, *Chips Barber*

Other Titles About This Area

Torquay, *Chips Barber* • Paignton, *Chips Barber* • Brixham, *Chips Barber*
Torbay in Colour – Torquay Paignton Brixham, *Chips Barber*
From Brixham… With Love, *Chips Barber*
The Ghosts of Brixham, *Graham Wyley*
The Ghosts of Berry Pomeroy Castle, *Deryck Seymour*
Pictures of Paignton, Parts I, II and III, *Peter Tully*
Cockington, *Jo Connell* • Colourful Cockington, *Chips Barber*

For a current list please send an SAE to
Obelisk Publications, 2 Church Hill, Pinhoe, Exeter EX4 9ER

Plate Acknowledgements:
All pictures supplied by Dave K. James apart from page 6 (top) supplied by Mrs Gilder.

This book is dedicated to the memory of Dave James' late mother, Hazel, and his mother-in-law, Ada

First published in 1995, reprinted in 2006 by
Obelisk Publications, 2 Church Hill, Pinhoe, Exeter, Devon
Designed by Chips and Sally Barber
Typeset by Sally Barber
Printed in Great Britain by
Avocet Press, Cullompton, Devon

BRIXHAM

of Yesteryear

Part II

Dave James is 'Brixham through and through', a man who loves the town where he was born and who has spent many years collecting pictures of the port. Almost all the ones featured in this second edition of "Brixham of Yesteryear" are from his extensive collection. The people of Brixham are also greatly interested in their town's history, so I have had no hesitation in publishing more pictures to evoke further memories.

Almost inevitably some views are similar to ones already presented in other publications, but there will always be subtle differences, even in these, and I have striven to include many scenes that are very different from anything that has been published before in a bid to avoid unnecessary repetition.

We start this second sequence of pictures with this view of the Outer Pier, from a postcard posted on 12 August 1912. The vessel in the centre is the *King Edward*, a ferry that regularly plied across Tor Bay. Look at the lack of development on the far side of the harbour. The water inside the harbour, as seen in this picture, is less choppy than that outside.

Here we have two views taken at Overgang. In the top picture it is possible to spy the Breakwater in the distance. The wall on the left hand side of the view has long since gone and there are flats on the right side of the scene; apart from that, not much has changed!

The older part of lower Brixham is a maze of narrow lanes, ill-suited to the rigours of modern traffic. The pedestrian needs to be fit for there are few places to match Brixham for the number of steps about and above the town. Most tourists are content to wander the flatter parts of Brixham, but those with alpine tendencies would enjoy a ramble along the alleys of Brixham's colourful, quaint back streets.

The postcard above was captioned "Brixham. Free Car Park." Whatever next? It's hard to imagine any such municipal benevolence these days. The former limestone quarry has been a useful additional parking place for a compact town with barely enough room to accommodate the crowds that come on fine days in high summer. Since this picture was taken, industrial buildings have been built on the space at the right hand side of this view.

The picture to the left was taken between this car park and the harbour and shows the former site of a paint factory, which took advantage of the ochre that occurred here. The ochre was dried in a pan kiln, then rolled and crushed to a fine powder. It was then mixed with varnishes and various thinners. This substance was found in even greater abundance on the north side of St Mary's Bay. Locally made paint, with rust-proofing properties, was made in Brixham and was in great demand far afield. The Victoria Falls Bridge, over the mighty Zambezi River, was painted with Brixham paint. This group of buildings has now been replaced by flats.

The picture above was a faint and frail affair, but is clearly recognisable as a part of Berry Head Road. It shows Breakwater House, and the way the picture has been taken makes it appear that it is on the edge of a steep cliff– but this is a trick of the eye for the road is between the houses and the water. Whether or not the caves underneath went back quite as far must fall into the realms of local knowledge.

Below is a picture postcard of Bolton Cross from an age when traffic was sparse and when the pace of life must have been much gentler.

How fortunes change! This pair of pictures is a reminder that the Northcliffe (Tel. No. Brixham 100), was a wonderful hotel, with one of the best views in the whole of Torbay. The hotel later closed, became derelict and was boarded up. To add insult to injury it was razed to the ground by fire. These pictures were taken in happier times. It was a private hotel and advertised itself in the local guide as "Brixham's Leading Hotel." Mrs Silley, resident proprietress, ran a fine hotel that had a vita glass sun lounge, 'hot and cold water in bedrooms' and 'moderate charges'.

Another building to have seen change, but which has survived, is the Mission Church of St Peter the Fisherman. It was erected in 1874 at the very precise cost of £2,212. It is built in what is described as the Early English style. Today the hymns listed on the display board will not be heard as the interior, which had seating for 350 worshippers, has been 'converted' into flats. The last service took place in 1977.

The view below looks towards the church, right of centre, from the other side of the harbour.

The picture above is a closer look at the Overgang and Furzeham area and shows the character of Brixham as a place with steep-sided hills and tiers of buildings peering over each other, clinging to the limestone.

Below is an old picture that may revive memories for those who knew the sheltered Fishcombe Cove in the days when it looked like this. This photo was taken long before large national companies invaded the great British seaside with massive holiday camps. Most people were restricted to the occasional day visit to the beach, unless, of course, they were fortunate enough to live at the coast.

Over the years tourism has become a major facet in Brixham's economy; the annual influx of visitors generates income for local businesses and creates a variety of summer jobs. But there have been consequences, for the hills in and around the port have been covered in camps. These pictures have their value in that they show two of the main holiday parks, St Mary's Bay (above) and Dolphin (below) opened in 1938, in an age when the expectations of the accommodation were a lot less grand than is expected these days. Brixham has many beaches and it has been said that, whatever the wind direction, a beach devotee can find at least one that will be sheltered from the wind. In the view opposite is St Mary's Bay (Mudstone Sands), the largest, which faces east, and enjoys the morning sun and turns its back on the prevailing westerly winds. This picture postcard, complete with the old refreshment hut seen in the left foreground, shows the view from the Sharkham Point side of the bay looking towards Durl Head.

E

The stretch of coastline between Kingswear and Brixham's Berry Head is wonderful. In the top view the camera is pointed from Berry Head towards Sharkham Point. A distinct cloud of smoke can be seen wafting heavenwards. This is no indigenous tribe of 'red indians' sending smoke signals, but is the former rubbish tip. Below is the familiar landmark of the lighthouse at Berry Head, known to many as "Captain Hoare's Baby" after the man who campaigned to have it erected on this two-hundred-foot-high headland. For almost sixty years, up to 1965, the light was maintained by men called Bowden, father and son, for 28 years and 31 years respectively.

The top picture shows the home of the Reverend Henry Francis Lyte.The hymn-writing Lyte has been the subject of many multi-view postcards (the bottom picture is typical) highlighting his connections with the port.

Arthur Mee wrote this of the great man in his book *Devon* in 1938: *Every day the bells of this church ring out the tunes of three of Henry Lyte's hymns, the one at eventide being always the imperishable hymn, 'Abide With Me'. Frail and tired he looked as he walked that autumn evening in 1847 from his church of All Saints, up the steep little streets to his home on Berry Head. The house is still there, snug at the foot of a woody combe facing Torbay. He had preached his last sermon though he did not know it, and the sailors who doffed their woollen caps as he passed would have found it hard to hide their emotion had they guessed the truth, for they loved this wan ghost of a man.*

BRIXHAM.

ALL SAINTS' CHURCH.

THE REVEREND
HENRY FRANCIS LYTE
Author of
"ABIDE WITH ME"

BERRY HEAD HOUSE

Abide with me; fast falls the eventide;
The darkness deepens; Lord, with me abide;
When other helpers fail and comforts flee,
Help of the helpless, O abide with me.

Mee went on to add: *He was weary and ill. In his mind were still ringing the words spoken to Jesus by his disciples on the road to Emmaus, Abide with us, for it is towards evening, and the day is far spent... It is thought that he sat down and wrote the hymn that which men everywhere have sung in hours of great emotion. Our men were heard singing it in France, and sometimes, when they stopped, the Germans in their trenches would take up the refrain.*

Here we have two views showing All Saints Church, rising above the rooftops. The one above has the Strand on the bottom right, whilst the bottom picture shows the buildings along the Quay on the middle right.

There are far fewer picture postcards of Brixham's Fore Street than the harbour or Berry Head, for it's not such a striking view. However, here are two from a pre-motor car age when there was no need to pedestrianise thoroughfares of this type. The one above was a postcard posted to London on a hot August day in 1907 to a Miss B. Head. We know that her Christian name was Beattie and not Berry! The upright picture was sent the following year, also to London, and the sender said that the weather was dull, but still much better than the London fog!

Most of the shops in the Fore Street of yesteryear were family-run businesses and the author of the 1929 *Bell's Pocket Guide to Devon* went as far as to say that: "The visitor to Brixham does not expect the sophistications of Torquay..." However, in another guide book published in 1899, *The Book of Fair Devon*, it states that: "The town is well paved, drained and lighted; its water supply is of the best quality and extensive sanitary arrangements have recently been effected." Can't say 'fairer' than that!

The picture shows the part of Brixham that has dramatically changed over the years, with the boat yards and other maritime industries giving way to homes of various shapes and sizes, as the waterfront views make them an attractive proposition. However, they were not built without great debate and a veritable cauldron of controversy. Many argued that the quaint narrow streets of Brixham should not be subjected to any significant increase in traffic generated by an influx of newcomers. Perhaps it's a pity that the

Torbay Paint company, whose logo included those immortal words "Don't 'ee Forget Torbay Paint lasts longest!", are not still around, for a fair amount of yellow paint must get used along the many narrow streets of the town and could have been a 'nice little earner' for the company. This photograph was taken a great many years ago at a time when there was much more green space in and around Brixham: the population has grown steadily since this was taken.

The statue of William of Orange has starred in a great number of picture postcard views. Here are four more, all different in their own way. Two of them have small boys climbing on the cannons, but the photographer has 'fired them' from the other two pictures. The mandatory seagull, that always seems to be standing on William's head, seems to have gone missing as well.

The picture below shows the extent of the fish market, stretching a considerable way along the quayside, always a scene of great, early morning activity. To the right can be seen many tall masts and the sails of the Brixham fleet in all their splendour rising high above the pier.

The visitors' guide book for 1933 contains an advert for Alfred S. Trant, who was an Ironmonger & Ship Chandler opposite the statue of William of Orange. The firm was an agent for many ranges and boasted specialities that included 'William of Orange Brass Ware'. Next left to Brokenshire, on the right side of the picture, it is possible to pick out part of the word 'institute'. This was the Fishermen's Institute and there is a fine picture in *Brixham of Yesteryear* (part one) showing it much more clearly.

The very nature of the waterfront buildings, found in the perimeter around Brixham's harbour, has changed considerably in recent decades. The above view of the Strand will bear this out, for amusement arcades are now found there: the Ironmonger in the above scene has become one, and the engineers on the left, seen in part only, this being Prout's Garage, is yet another.

The picture below shows Brixham's inner harbour as it looked in 1922. How times have changed!

The top picture opposite is taken in Berry Head Road, before the erection of the War Memorial cross. There are also no double yellow lines, as nothing like this sort of restriction was needed when the amount of traffic passing along this narrow road was negligible.

The picture below is taken from the Breakwater, looking back towards the red-sailed fleet and Brixham town. The inter-war years were tough ones for Brixham's fleet and there were many reasons for the decline. One of the more unusual was the loss of fishing equipment snagged on wrecks caused by enemy submarines. The *Devon and Exeter Gazette*, in December 1928, stated that there were 140 such wrecks between Start Point and Portland Bill. They went on to add that Brixham's fleet had gone from some 350 vessels down to fewer than a hundred, and (a sign of really hard times) that no apprentices were being taken on. Of course the Government and the Ministry of Agriculture and Fisheries were asked for assistance, but the responses received were not the ones the Brixham fishermen wanted to hear.

This is the harbour as it was seen by the purchaser of this postcard who sent it in mid August 1927. The one below, capturing the flavour of Brixham, was probably bought, and definitely sent, in July 1912, from Exeter to Willand near Cullompton. It is very doubtful whether you could buy a Brixham view card in Exeter these days and vice-versa!

The small picture in the bottom left corner of the bottom picture postcard is of Fore Street, the same picture as the upper one on page 15 of this book. They must have had a limited selection, but by putting it into a circle cunningly used it again!

Showing Brixham's Fish Market, this card was sent to the other side of the world in 1912. The recipient lived in Wellington, New Zealand, but the card has found its way home more than four score years later and was acquired at a postcard fair for hundreds of times its original face value.

The picture below shows the fish being prepared for sale. Quite a little crowd of cap-wearing local people have assembled for this photograph. The photographer had to keep them as still as possible for a sharp picture. However, somebody, to the right of centre, has moved, resulting in a blur that has assured them of perpetual anonymity.

In *The Book of Fair Devon*, published in 1899, it had this to say of Brixham's fish market: *The Fish Market on the south side of the harbour, on which tons of fish are sold almost every day, affords infinite interest and amusement, and the scene presents itself on anything like a busy day as lively and varied. Great, hearty, robust, "baccy" smoking men in blue jerseys and big sea boots are busy bringing their fish to market, and the work of selling the various lots proceeds with rapidity.*

The above view was taken from Prospect Road, and shows the old Ice Factory on the right side of the picture. Bay View is at the top right of the scene. Below, we see what must be one of the biggest vessels to enter the Inner Harbour, on a postcard published by Stevens and Stevens who had their premises in Fore Street. The firm was also a stationers and bookseller that, as a sideline, also dabbled in Berlin wools, worsteds and fancy needlework – fancy that!

In the above picture, from more than a century ago, the tide is out, so many of the vessels are leaning gently onto the mud, a primeval sort of ooze with its own peculiar smell, fortunately not communicated to us! In 1937 so much mud had accumulated at the bottom of the harbour that it was deemed necessary to enlist the services of the Great Western Railway's steam dredger, *Graball* to grab as much of this foul stuff as it could. As a result some 3,500 tons were dredged and later dumped outside the International Limits. This made the berths at the inner pier some five feet deeper.

Below is another very old picture, this time showing the trawler, *Sirdar*, berthed at the Middle Pier.

The harbour always looks better when the tide is in. Below, the gentleman on the left, with the cigarette in his mouth, is the late George Webber who was a mackerel fisherman of great repute. He once rod caught a fine specimen fish of almost five pounds. Behind him is BM 10, a trawler called *David Allen,* whose name had nothing to do with the Irish comedian of the same name. It was a vessel that originally came from Fleetwood in Lancashire.

For generations people have preferred to make the journey from Torquay to Brixham by ferry, and, if truth be told, it would be a much more pleasant option today as the traffic around the Bay makes it something of a chore to drive between the two places. The above picture, from a great many years ago, shows a number of visitors who have done such a journey, their marine conveyance being the SS *Pioneer*. Below, the postcard shows the view looking north-westwards towards Torquay, but the card is the sort that doesn't have any distant detail. Strangely, when it was posted in September 1913 to an address in Moss Side, Manchester, it bore no message whatsoever.

Many people are drawn to Brixham for its harbour and its quaint narrow streets. The picture above shows the end of Fore Street as it runs down to meet the Strand by the harbour. The next short sequence of pictures features more distant parts, but the continued outward growth of the town means that they aren't quite so far from Brixham as they used to be. The picture below was captioned "School and Post Office, Churston, near Brixham" and the postcard on which it appeared was posted on 8 January 1907 to thank a friend in Torquay for sending a photo as a special surprise New Year present. Cards were common forms of cheap communication when telephones were rare.

The justification for including two old views of Broadsands lies in the fact that Brixham can almost be seen in the distance, even though the town is nestled nicely out of sight. If change is what most of this book is about then these two scenes are more than qualified to be included, as both views have changed with the whole area of Broadsands now developed into acres of attractive houses. The top picture shows a car park on this side of the railway viaduct. The lower picture shows how undeveloped the beach area was when this picture was taken, a marsh existing where the present car park is now located.

One of these postcards was sent by somebody on holiday from the North of England, who reckoned that when they first saw the harbour area in Brixham, it bore an uncanny resemblance to Whitby in Yorkshire. In the bottom picture, originally published by H. Rawlings of the Quay, it is possible to spot a charabanc on the far side of the Inner Harbour. Charles Gregory had this to say in his *Brixham, in Devonia*, published long, long ago, about some of the housing in the lower part of the town: *Fishermen are, as a rule, very careless of the picturesque, but here they have been unable to destroy it. Notwithstanding the great change that has been brought about by the improved style of dwellings in which most of the smack owners and a great number of the well-to-do classes now reside on the hill sides, there still exists in the lower part of town, many dwellings of very primitive styles of architecture pitched here and there, in a 'higgledy piggledy' fashion, rejoicing in an air of supreme indifference as to what those of more modern date may think of them. Lovers of the ancient will find much food for reflection in wending their way through the many defiles in these quarters.*

It may appear to be the same view that appears on page 3 of this book, but if you compare the two, closely, you will see that there are some considerable differences, from the building of new houses to the covered boat-building yards at Upham's on the far side of the harbour. This picture is thus several years later. There are even newer railings in the foreground! However, much of what has appeared has gone again, so if you had made an eighty-year-long blink, you would have missed most of it!

Sitting by the harbour is an activity many enjoy, when they have the time, for it is an ever-changing picture. Vessels come and go as they have done for many generations. The tides ebb and flow with monotonous regularity. However, the fortunes of the fishing industry also rise and fall, fluctuating for all sorts of reasons. Brixham has seen it all before and its fishermen know that these days it isn't a simple case of netting enough fish. I wonder what the two men sat on the upturned boat would think if they knew how things would turn out many years later...

We have come to the end of this particular sequence of pictures of a much-changed port and town. There is still, though, that pervading smell of fish, although it's often joked that they catch more tourists these days. Whatever the situation, or the truth of it, we finish this portion of photographic nostalgia with those famous red sails, often in the sunset, so tall and strikingly graceful, sailing into the memories of a second edition of *Brixham of Yesteryear*. Hope you enjoyed the trip – don't forget to look out for Part III!